# Atlas
## Shrugged

## A Summary of
## Ayn Rand's Classic Novel

# Trisha Lively

**Atlas Shrugged 100 page summaries**
copyright © by 100 page summaries.

ISBN: 978-1-939370-00-6

Library of Congress Cataloging-in-Publication Data

Lively, Trisha
Atlas Shrugged A Summary of Ayn Rand's Classic Novel/Trisha Lively

This publication is designed to provide accurate and authoritative information in regard to the subject matter covered. It is sold with the understanding that neither the author nor the publisher is registered experts in the subject matter discussed. If legal advice or other expert assistance is required, the services of a competent professional person should be sought.

# Table of Contents

# Short Summary

This book uses a railroad and a steel mill to reflect what is going on in the entire country and at times the world. We start off with a vibrant economy and a railroad business that has grown for three generations of the Taggart Family. But in these times things are slowing down. The world is separating into two camps: one side that produces value and products and one side that uses as much as they can without contributing or paying for what they take (moochers or looters).

The looters are able to take things by using double talk and corrupting patriotic concepts to pass laws. What they do is say a law is for the good of all and to ensure freedom, while actually the law is only going to be good for the looters and is taking away freedoms. They take more and more, and pass more and more laws until it becomes very difficult for businesses to operate.

As companies start to close down, their owners seem to retire and then vanish. At the same time, there are fewer products and fewer replacement parts. The economy now starts to spiral downward faster. In response, the moochers make it illegal to change jobs, quit or even hire people – this is in an attempt to keep things the same so that things don't get worse. But they do get worse.

At the same time the economy is getting worse, the main characters are struggling with concepts such as sex, love, basic values, what is moral, earning a living, freedom and the free market. These serious topics are dealt with in a very realistic way; like real-life things aren't always just black and white, and decisions are not easy to make. Often one character will make a snide remark that only the reader understands, like an inside joke. A plane chase, ray shields, a gun fight and a handsome pirate carry the story along as their world rushes toward an economic collapse.

While the good guys fight to keep the world going, even more people seem to vanish into thin air. The moochers feel like they are losing control, so they develop a sound weapon that can pulverize people and buildings alike. They make a new attempt to get control of everything by confiscating things in the name of the government, which is really just them.

A handful of brave people are fighting back, but it may be too late. Will NYC become the biggest ghost town ever known? Will America have slaves again? Will love win out?

# PART ONE:

## NON-CONTRADICTION

# Part 1:
# Chapter 1 – THE THEME

## What Happens?

The grey streets of New York City provide the opening background. Eddie Willers is a middle-aged man heading in to speak to James (Jim) Taggart, the President of Taggart Transcontinental Railroad – what used to be the gold standard for rail companies. Eddie is carrying the news that one of their divisions, the Rio Norte Line, has had yet another train wreck. Eddie, like the Taggart Transcontinental, has been entwined with the Taggart family for generations. Eddie grew up with James and his sister, Dagny, on their country estate.

This evening, Eddie is trying to prod James into coming up with a solution and taking *any* kind of action which will help to save the Rio Norte Line. Not only is the rail falling apart, but now there is fierce competition from another rail company: the Phoenix-Durango. One main solution would be to purchase new rail material and lay replacement track down. James placed an order over a year ago with a friend (Orren Boyle) who keeps pushing back the delivery date. Rearden Steel could fill the order immediately, but James has a personal dislike for Hank Rearden, so he will not use Rearden Steel. As he whines with inaction, the railroad is crumbling around him.

Dagny enters the scene riding a coach in one of her own trains, The Comet. She is listening to a young brakeman hum a symphony so perfectly composed that for a while she thinks she is listening to a recording. She recognizes the style of the music and asks the brakeman who wrote it: Richard Halley. He tells her it is his Fifth Concerto. Yet only four have been on the market. When Dagny questions him on this, he at once shuts up and goes back to work. We are left with the mystery of how an efficient young rail worker knows an unpublished masterpiece of music so well as to hum it perfectly.

Dagny has no time to follow up, as The Comet comes to a halt on a rail spur. They were directed off the main rail line to a side line to wait by a red warning signal. As Dagny reveals to the engineer that she is the Vice-President of Operations of Taggart Transcendental and demands to know why the express train has stopped, she finds that there seems to be no reason for it. No one knows why they are waiting, but they all continue waiting because none of them seems to know how to find an answer. Finally Dagny orders them to "Proceed with caution to the next signal. If it's in order, proceed to the main track." She determines to fire the superintendent of the Ohio Division who has been responsible for these types of delays in the past. She plans to advance a young Owen Kellogg to this position as soon as she reaches NYC.

Dagny flops on the arm of a chair in her brother's office. Eddie is her assistant and is there so "She never had to explain anything to him afterwards." Dagny informs her brother she has ordered rail made out of a new material called Rearden metal. She claims it will be even stronger than steel. James protests. Finally, after Dagny agrees she will take the blame if anything goes wrong or the Board is displeased, James stops arguing with his sister and the order will stand as placed. Dagny leaves for her own office calling Owen Kellogg in to offer him a job. She finds he has determined to quit working for Taggart Transcendental and there is nothing she can offer him to entice him to stay.

## Analysis:

Ayn Rand set the opening for this large book in NYC, just as the sun was setting and further elaborating on the decay in the city as the world grows darker. She speaks of broken glass and the metal sky. The first character to speak is a bum. The next is Eddie Willers who hands the bum a dime for coffee. Eddie is an ambiguous character at this point. He seems to be intelligent and to want to "Do the right thing." Yet he is a quiet character who moves in the shadows of the more dynamic characters and Eddie allows the others to make decisions.

Eddie is first shown trying to convince James Taggart to purchase Rearden Steel in order to save an entire branch of their railroad. All James has to say is that he doesn't want to discuss it, and Eddie drops it, trying to work another angle to motivate the president of the company to do something to save the family business. Even as Ms. Rand describes Eddie, it comes off as just average.

On the other hand, she describes James with strong words that leave no doubt that one should not respect a person such as James Taggart – words and phrases such as, "Petulant mouth," "Thin hair clinging to a bald forehead," "Gawkiness of a lout," and "Flesh of his face was pale and soft." His mannerisms are just as offensive because he doesn't hold anyone's gaze (shifty eyes) and he rarely raises his head; he just stares up through heavy eyelids. In keeping with this description, his decisions, or lack thereof, are distasteful. He doesn't want to make any decisions; he tries desperately to change the subject when he is pressed to make a specific decision. If pressed harder, he finally points out that he can't be held responsible for his decisions.

Dagny Taggart is the opposite of her brother. She is quick to look a person in the eye. She listens to the situation and makes a solid decision, ready to move on to the next problem. Ms. Rand takes time to point out that Dagny is a lovely person, but not caught up in fashion. She is more concerned about getting to the office than getting the wrinkles out of her clothes. She has nice legs, long brown hair and intelligent grey eyes, but when duty calls she doesn't think twice about grabbing an old coat and catching a ride on a public train.

## Key Takeaways:

*"Who is John Galt?"* is the very first sentence and the very last sentence of this chapter. This question is asked by a bum, by Eddie to himself and by a good worker. It is not explained in the first chapter. It is used almost like we would say, "It is what it is." Although we assume this phrase will be explained later in the book, for now we are ironically left to wonder ourselves, "Who is John Galt?"

The sun is setting on NYC, and the images that are weaved into this chapter seem to imply that the sun is setting on human civilization as we know it. Even the typewriters are not made of strong metal anymore and break soon after use. Once the old metal typewriters all break, there will be a crisis – just as once the buildings, railroads and oil wells that have been created break down; it does not seem like there will be any replacements that will do the jobs half as well.

Ms. Rand uses the imagery of skyscrapers to show how much people have achieved, and how it can crumble if we do not work to keep our society strong and vibrant. This plays off the Halley Concerto, the Fifth one being hummed by a rail worker. Dagny recognizes pieces of past work that Richard Halley has written in this new piece of music, tying in that talented people build up to masterpieces and also build upon the good work that others have done before them; that amazing achievement can be made, as long as we are moving forward, as long as we work toward our masterpieces.

In opposition to this stand the bulk of the people – people who are afraid to take any risk because they are afraid to be blamed if anything goes wrong. Since they take no risk, nothing new is created. Since they take no risk, nothing gets repaired. Their world is crumbling around them and they pretend not to see it because they are afraid to take action and face the possibility that they may not do something perfectly.

# Part 1:
# Chapter 2 – THE CHAIN

## What Happens?

The chapter plunges right into the heat and power of a steel mill. Rearden Steel is pouring their first heat of Rearden metal; heat being what is referred to as a new batch of steel being made. Henry (Hank) Rearden is watching his metal workers pour the liquid metal. He has just realized that ten years of hard work on this new metal has finally paid off – ten years that family, friends and others in his industry all said were wasted and a new metal could never be formed.

Hank walks home alone in the dark. He is toying with a chain bracelet he made for his wife from this new metal. He has taken a slice of the masterpiece he created and made a gift for Lillian Rearden. He walks into his house late for dinner and no one greets him until he walks further into the living room. His mother, brother, wife and a family friend, Paul Larkin, are all gathered around; none seem to realize he just poured the first heat of Rearden metal, his goal for the last ten years.

The family scolds him for being late. They all carry on a boring conversation. Lillian teases him mean-spiritedly about making an appointment with him in order to plan a party and assure he will be there. The date is set: their wedding anniversary. His brother attempts to guilt him into giving money to his current pet charity. Hank wants to spread the happiness he feels about his new metal, so he agrees. This gesture is met with more scolding that he doesn't do this more often.

Hank finally has a good opportunity to give the gift to his wife. She holds it up pinched between two fingers. Hank is made fun of for giving her a lump of a bracelet instead of a diamond bracelet. She calls the gesture sweet and charming while at the same time dropping the chain bracelet on a table. Seems that nothing Hank does is going to make his family happy. Hank is confused because he tries and fails with his family.

## Analysis:

This chapter seems to connect back to a theme of not wanting to take action. The family members, and even Paul, seem to be weighted down and unable to do anything but talk. They resent Hank, the very person whose work allows them to be lazy. It is perhaps a subconscious way for them to reflect the guilt and blame from themselves onto the only person who has the strength to take it – whether it is fair or not. Their emotions are all superficial and immediate: what will others think; who was over for dinner; you work too hard and you are always late.

Philip Rearden is younger than Hank, yet he is sickly and whines, and cannot hold down a job. He lives off his brother's money and says he works for "charity" organizations, not realizing he himself is receiving charity. Hank's mother is open about her disappointment in her eldest son, concerned with social manners and nothing about his interests or achievements. She also lives off his money. Lillian Rearden is a lovely wife, yet she is languid and slow. Her method of self-defense is to zing Hank with sharp words in the form of teasing. Since she does it constantly, we know she is cruel – Hank does not see this yet.

Their inaction and false behavior is in direct contrast to Hank, who actually feels deep emotions. Hank feels connected with the earth and with his own power. They seem to bounce around in a fog. Hank has produced something and is proud of it. They just want to impress others. Hank is happy and tried to give them the benefit of the doubt, thinking he must not judge them harshly because he doesn't understand; thinking that perhaps they have the same type of passion and love that he does, just for different things. He couldn't be more wrong.

## Key Takeaways:

Only a worker in the mill gave Rearden any acknowledgement for the masterpiece of creating Rearden metal – it was nonverbal. He glanced up at Hank during the first heat pour and grinned at his boss. Rearden smiled in answer. It was the only salute he had received. Then he started back for his office, once again a figure with an expressionless face. Hank does not wear his emotions on his sleeve to prove he has them. He has deep emotions, yet he lets logic and planning carry the day.

The family friend, Paul Larkin, is somewhat like Eddie Willers: he sees the greatness in Hank and respects it – one of the few who lets that knowledge come to the forefront of their minds, but yet they don't speak it out loud. They still choose to live in the midst of the cruel masses. Not believing the lazy others, but not strong enough to break away from the mob. Paul makes an attempt to warn Hank of a problem with his paid lobbyist in Washington D.C. but his warning is too vague. He then slumps down, giving up, telling himself he has done his duty and warned Hank, when he knows he didn't really come out and say exactly what he needed to say.

The rest of the family keep up a chorus all evening: "It's no use trying to do things for you – you don't appreciate it." Yet how can anything they do be appreciated when it is done reproachfully and with resentment? Or if it is done for the person doing it rather than the one receiving it? This is what Hank is up against in his own home.

Hank offers a true gift, one made of a material he is proud of, to his wife. His intention is only to share his joy. It is received with the opposite result, his wife mocking him for being rich yet making her a gift from a material that bridges and pots are made of. She accuses him of using his wealth to keep her chained to him. The bracelet is seen by her as a symbol of his power over her. It was seen by Hank as a symbol of sharing and joy. No one will hear what he is saying or accept his reasons. They all resent him for not needing them. Since they need *him* to support them so they don't have to work, they push all the blame back on Hank.

# Part 1:
# Chapter 3 – THE TOP AND THE BOTTOM

## What Happens?

We start at the top of a skyscraper in NYC, with the lowest of moral people. James Taggart and Orren Boyle are having a meeting over drinks in an exclusive bar. The bar is on top of the world and looks like a dingy cramped cellar. Paul Larkin and Wesley Mouch have joined the powerful men. The discussion is never straightforward; just hints that they should press the government to take ownership away from the only steel mills and oil wells that are doing well – all for the good of the whole society. When they have bullied their way to an agreement, the meeting ends and they emerge into the sunset, surprised that the world is not dark.

Dagny Taggart is in her office late that night, thinking back on her childhood and how she always knew she would run the company someday. How much joy she took in working her way up from a simple entry-level job to doing the job of Vice-President of Operations before she ever had the position appointed to her by the board. She is proud of all she has learned and earned.

James bursts into her office because he learned over that dark meeting that only two trains were running on their Mexican Line; he was embarrassed in front of his cronies because he didn't know this. Dagny laughs at him and tells him he would know it if he read his reports; it has been that way for over three months. Dagny knows they are losing money on the San Sebastián line and has pulled every good piece of equipment out of Mexico, leaving only the dregs and a wood-fired engine. James has bet millions of dollars that a mine owned by Francisco d'Anconia will produce big, so he built the rail line and invested heavily in the stock of the San Sebastián mines. He also had relied on the assurances of the Mexican Government that they will let the rail and the mine remain as private-owned property – although everything else in the entire country has become government owned. Dagny knows this won't last; James insisted he was promised it would.

We end the chapter at the bottom, in a basement cafeteria that is bright and cheerful with white tiles and chromium counters. Eddie Willers sits next to a mysterious rail worker. he never asks for his name but often has lunch or dinner with this man whose clothes are grease-stained. Eddie feels at ease with this hardworking man, and often shares things he would never say out loud to anyone else. This night the worker asks him questions about Dagny. Eddie answers with how hardworking she is and his belief that she will save Taggart Transcontinental. The worker asks what she does when not working. Eddie answers that she listens to the music of Richard Halley – that is the only thing other than the rail that she seems to love.

## Analysis:

Ms. Rand is painting a picture of contrast and hypocrisy. The morally corrupt James and Orren cry for the government to take over two specific businesses because they are not strong enough to compete; they see no contradiction in then saying that this would be to preserve a free economy. They meet in a shady place, have to lean forward and talk like conspirators – because that is what they are. A telling phrase is this: "The only justification of private property," said Orren Boyle, "is public service." This is certainly a continuation of his refusing to let himself see the true meaning of those words.

Meanwhile, Dagny hides nothing. She explains exactly why she pulled equipment from the Mexican line and even laughs when James tries to bully her. She walks in the open and looks people right in the eye. A hard worker eats in a bright open cafeteria and Eddie speaks openly and eagerly with this hardworking man. The two worlds couldn't be further apart – yet they exist in the same space and time.

## Key Takeaways:

The lazy looters are still afraid of the few who work hard. They are afraid, but never call it that and never say exactly why they are afraid – they just swirl in excuses and complaints. "When everybody agrees," Taggart's voice suddenly went shrill, "when people are unanimous, how does one man dare to dissent? By what right? That's what I want to know – by what right?"

A key event that is introduced in this chapter is Francisco d'Anconia and the San Sebastián copper mines. Francisco has convinced the American men to invest very heavily in his mines – all resting on the rumor of his supposed good luck and that he has always been successful. They buy into this, yet get the same excuses that Orren gives to James (remember, Orren has not filled the rail order for over a year): the orders for copper are not fulfilled so far because they are still setting up the mine. It will all come as soon as humanly possible. We also learn that Dagny once knew Francisco and has not spoken to him in years. We do not learn any more at this time; we are left with a mystery again.

This chapter starts at the top of NYC in a room that looks like a cellar (the bottom) and with people who are the pits. It ends with Dagny pressing forward against all odds, with no one agreeing with her and with a hardworking man having a bright conversation with Eddie.

# Part 1:
# Chapter 4 – THE IMMOVABLE MOVERS

## What Happens?

Dagny Taggart has just returned from a business trip to NJ to see why a supplier is late with her diesel engines. "She had learned nothing: neither the reason for the delays nor any indication of the date the diesel engines would be produced. The president of the company had talked to her for two hours. But none of his answers had connected to any of her questions." Now she learns that another competent person has closed his business and gone: McNamara, the contractor she has used in Mexico and the one she was planning to use in Colorado (the Rio Norte Line). Gone with no reason and no one knows where.

Trying to get some relaxation, she listens to Halley's Fourth Concerto – in this she can appreciate masterpiece-level work from another; she can take joy in listening. She thinks back to the last time the composer was seen, just after an opera he wrote was revived. It had opened and closed the first day nineteen years before the second showing – closed due to boos and bad reviews. This time she was there and it got thunderous applause. Halley had just stared at the audience. Then he retired, sold his royalties and just ... disappeared.

Francisco d'Anconia makes headlines in the papers connected to a scandalous divorce where the wife, together with her lover, Francisco, shot her husband-to-be. (This is taking place during a time when divorce was not common.) The husband survives being shot and a messy divorce is now in play. The wife is dragging every little detail out for the papers to share; Francisco says nothing. James is sharing in a similar farce, being the lover of wealthy Betty Pope, for whom he has no feelings. It is just expected that he should connect with some wealthy female.

News reaches NYC that the Mexican Government has seized the mine and railroad. James takes credit for pulling out all the valuable equipment. Dagny doesn't care to mention she was the one who knew something would happen. Another business deal, **the Anti-Dog-Eat-Dog Rule**, is passed by the National Alliance of Railroads – a group of business owners all related to the railroad. This claimed to protect the welfare of the railroad and society by forcing new companies out of any market that the group decided to call "restricted," thereby allowing the looters to have full control of any rail line they think is profitable.

## Analysis:

Because of the Anti-Dog-Eat-Dog Rule, Dagny now has to have the Rearden metal rails laid down in Colorado in nine months as opposed to a year. This also means that the only competition, the Durango-Phoenix line, will be shut down and the owner, Conway, will be out of business. Dagny is furious that she has to be a part of this; however, the business owners in Colorado will now be depending on her and she must make it work.

## Key Takeaways:

"Nothing can make it moral to destroy the best." This is why Dagny is so furious about the Rule: it makes her feel like she is a looter/thief. She is sad when Ellis Wyatt comes into her office and assumes she is like the rest of her brother's friends. He wants to make sure the rail will deliver his oil. He is demanding competence from her: "I have no interest in discussions and intentions. I expect transportation...You expect to feed off me while you can and to find another carcass to pick dry after you have finished mine. That is the policy of most of mankind today. So here is my ultimatum: it is now in your power to destroy me; I may have to go; but if I go, I'll make sure that I take all the rest of you along with me."

Dagny wishes she could talk to him as he is one of the few intelligent people she knows, but only says, "You will get the transportation you need, Mr. Wyatt."

This is what the strong can do. They can assess the situation and they know what can or cannot be done. The rest of the world can depend on any promise they make. Rearden makes a similar statement to Dagny when he promises she will have his rails early so she can run in Colorado.

Who is immovable here? The looters who refuse to work and refuse to see talent? Or the strong people who do their chosen work no matter what the world throws at them?

# Part 1:
# Chapter 5 – THE CLIMAX OF THE D'ANCONIAS

## What Happens?

News comes to Dagny that the Mexican Government has discovered that the San Sebastián mines were worthless. Eddie sets an appointment for her to see Francisco; he says, "Any time you wish" – as opposed to refusing to meet with James days earlier. As Dagny is walking to the posh Wayne-Falkland Hotel, she thinks back to her childhood.

Francisco's family was very rich and came from Spanish royalty. An ancestor had to flee for his life because he spoke his mind during the Spanish Inquisition. He settled in Argentina and built an empire out of mining. Young Francisco stays at the Taggart Estate one month each summer. Eddie often joins them in exploring the world but James never does. Francisco calls Dagny Slug and she starts to call him Frisco. At first they are both just annoying each other with the nicknames, then they become endearing. Slug means "a great fire in a locomotive firebox" and was how Frisco looked at Dagny. Over the years their childhood friendship grew to a romantic attraction. They became lovers when they were both in college. Even then they would greet each other after months of not seeing or talking or writing with, "Hi, Slug!" and "Hi, Frisco!"

The world (the looters) was starting to beat Frisco down. He knew he couldn't continue on like he was doing. Though they had never said the words, he and Dagny loved each other fiercely. He knew what he was going to do would hurt her, and it hurt him even more thinking about it. At this time, we are left with a mystery as to what his plan is; he tries to give Dagny as much of an explanation as he can at the time: "Dagny, don't be astonished by anything I do ... or by anything I may ever do in the future." He wants her to be with him, but he knows she is not ready yet to see what his plan means. He is tortured that what he must do will disappoint her and perhaps make her hate him. They part. He turns into a rich playboy, exactly the opposite of the intelligent, driven, hard worker he was.

Now Dagny enters his hotel room. He is sprawled out on the floor. She takes a chair so he is looking up at her. She asks him why he really came to NYC. He laughs at her, impressed that she is the only one who thinks he may be there because of the mines and not the divorce scandal in the papers. She knows he knew it would end like this and he prompts her to try to figure out why ... but she can't see past just his amusement about taking the money of stockholders like James. She is still not ready and we are not shown Frisco's plan.

## Analysis:

Ms. Rand goes into great detail about how such a strong and committed love can grow between two intelligent people. She paints a picture so powerful that you can feel they are connected at every level. It is a great and true love, and this is why it hurt both of them when it ended, Dagny in confusion and Frisco in abject sadness that Dagny was not ready to come with him yet. She contrasts this great love affair with mindless sex that happens when people have not taken the time to fall in love.

## Key Takeaways:

This chapter is one of the best love stories ever written, all contained in one long chapter. It does not contain the base betrayal or angst of breaking up and getting back together that many books contain today. It shows the joy and fun and partnership that two people can create. It is inspiring.

This chapter is also now opening the door to hints of what is to come. We know Frisco is intelligent, so we know he knew the mine was useless, yet he got the looters to invest their money and when the Mexican Government took it over, it hurt them financially. He hints to Dagny that it wasn't just to make those men lose money – although they lost millions. He hints that he must destroy Taggart Transcontinental (TT) and he will also destroy Ellis Wyatt. As a young man, he would have admired all that he now says he is out to destroy.

Dagny can't figure it out; she leaves but not before catching him off guard by asking if knows if Halley has written a Fifth Concerto. He is shocked into stillness. Then passes off the subject. We are left with the impression that he knows there is a Fifth Concerto and is keeping what he knows from Dagny.

# Part 1:
# Chapter 6 – THE NON-COMMERCIAL

## What Happens?

The day of Rearden's wedding anniversary party is here. Hank Rearden is not looking forward to it, but dresses formally and goes downstairs. Lillian has invited all manner of looter types, from hack musicians to philosophy professors to reporters. They carry on the most superficial and boring conversations and Hank tries to escape them by staring out the window at his steel mill. He feels like "an outcast among men" but tries for the sake of his wife to be pleasant. His mind wanders back to his work and a very good superintendent who resigned suddenly with no explanation. Then Francisco approaches him. Like Dagny, he is disgusted by the playboy ways and the wasting of money that he sees in Francisco's behavior. He is shocked when he realizes Francisco is speaking to him intelligently and with respect, and also seems to know what is really important to Hank. Still, Rearden is resisting liking this man and pushes back, demanding to know why Francisco has bothered to talk to him. The reply he gets is that Francisco wants to help him put words to his feelings and to understand Rearden. This is mysterious. While Rearden looks out at the lazy crowd, Francisco leaves him with a few pointed ideas: "I am calling your attention to the nature of those for whom you are working" and, "Why are you willing to carry them?"

Dagny has also attended the party – in a black gown with a bare shoulder – shocking since she is usually only seen in business suits. She tries to talk to Rearden all evening and is puzzled that he seems to be avoiding her. Throughout the last few chapters, the phrase, "Who is John Galt?" has been said occasionally. Tonight Dagny overhears it from a group of older ladies. She is startled when one says she knows who John Galt is! The lady weaves a tale of a yacht being sailed by John; he found the lost city of Atlantis! The city that "Was a place where hero-spirits lived in a happiness unknown to the rest of the earth. A place which only the spirits of heroes could enter." Since it was so perfect, one would no longer want to be anyplace else on earth – so John Galt sank his yacht and went down with his entire crew. Dagny scoffs at the story, Francisco laughs at her and says she doesn't know it, but the old woman was telling the truth. He moves off but watches Dagny the rest of the night – as Hank is also watching her.

Toward the end of the night, Dagny hears Halley's Fourth Concerto start to play – then it is morphed into a modern version, which the author describes as, "Torn apart, its holes stuffed with hiccoughs. The great statement of joy had become the giggling of a barroom." Francisco was looking right at Dagny's shocked face and laughing.

## Analysis:

Ms. Rand is showing here that the prattle of the looters is always actually mindless; that the leaders of the looters know what they are doing, at least on some level, and are cruel and dangerous. Lillian has dressed up in diamonds all over except for one arm, where she wears the chain bracelet. She has been saying to guests all night: "Why, no, it's not from a hardware store; it's a very special gift from my husband. Oh, yes, of course it's hideous. But don't you see? It's supposed to be priceless. Of course, I'd exchange it for a common diamond bracelet any time, but somehow nobody will offer me one for it, even though it is so very, very valuable. Why? My dear, it's the first thing ever made of Rearden metal."

We are introduced to two new concepts here. The first is a pirate called Ragnar Danneskjöld who is seizing ships filled with charity aid. No one knows what he does with the cargo. The second is that countries are now being referred to differently, as the People's State of France, and Norway, and even The People's State of England.

## Key Takeaways:

In the guise of democracy and freedom, a small group of looters is attempting to take over all governments. The newest movement from the looters is the **Equalization of Opportunity Bill**, which says that a person can only run one business – supposedly to give others a chance to run a business. Professor Pritchett says, "...I am in favor of a free economy. A free economy cannot exist without competition. Therefore, men must be forced to compete. Therefore, we must control men in order to force them to be free." When someone challenges that this is a contradiction, the response is that the person challenging this thinking is old-fashioned and not seeing the big picture; they are belittled and so, in order to not be embarrassed further, they nod and let their challenge to the idea drop.

A pattern is emerging in this chapter in terms of the people who attended Patrick Henry University. Many of the students who attended studied under Professor Hugh Akston, who has retired and seemed to disappear.

Hank ends the chapter with wondering why his wife married him and realizing that he has lost all interest in his wife (has for the last eight years) and we get the hint that he is attracted to Dagny and that this may be why he avoided her. He does not want to cheat on his wife; though he does not love her anymore, he respects the *title* of wife.

# Part 1:
# Chapter 7 – THE EXPLOITERS AND THE EXPLOITED

## What Happens?

Dagny is in Colorado overseeing the building of the new rail line. Hank Rearden visits to help design a bridge made of Rearden metal. Dagny has no clue he is attracted to her, but Hank finally admits it to himself. He still tries to keep his distance and only deal with her for work. When she returns to her office in NYC, Eddie tells her that the State Science Institute has undercut Rearden metal, and who knows when it may be stressed and fail. Since they can't find any scientific evidence, they played on hints and fear. The masses now won't ride over a bridge made of the new metal. Eddie laments to Dagny, "Why did that statement succeed? It's such an obvious smear-job, so obvious and so rotten. You'd think a decent person would throw it in the gutter ... how could they accept it? Didn't they read it? Didn't they see? Don't they think?"

Funders have left TT because they are still using the metal. Dagny demands that her brother go along with a plan she has: she will temporarily leave as VP in Taggart Transcendental and start her own rail line; build it like it should be and sell it back to TT – then take up her VP job again. Her brother makes her sign a paper that she promises to sell it back if it is successful and to take all the blame if it is not. In anger and amusement, Dagny decides to call her new rail the John Galt line. Dagny has to find funders for this new line. She asks Francisco, even begs him, but he will not come on board as a funder. She says she can't believe he is all gone because he still acts like he has his intelligence. Francisco gives her another hint by saying, "Contradictions do not exist. Whenever you think that you are facing a contradiction, check your premises. You will find that one of them is wrong." Yet he knows he can't tell her straight out what is going on – she is still not ready and it would hurt her. Instead, he says, "It is an answer which you must reach yourself."

Still in shock over the attack on the new metal, Dagny visits the Science Institute's head, Dr. Robert Stadler. He is old and tired and didn't know about the report. He disagrees with it, but says there is nothing he can do; he is funded by the government types that wanted that report. Dagny is disappointed as Dr. Stadler used to be a great man, used to teach at Patrick Henry University. He mentions three star students he and Hugh Akston taught there – the best he had ever known. One was Francisco d'Anconia, another was Ragnar Danneskjöld and he claims the third did not turn out notorious – but vanished without a trace.

The next blow from the looters is the passing of the Equalization of Opportunity Bill, which will force all the strong people into only owning one business. But since men like Rearden have an iron mine, and because no one else can deliver the iron to his steel mill, in effect it will ruin every industry that is still producing well. Rearden's lobbyist in Washington, Mr. Mouch, is not calling him back. In his despair, Rearden's brain still manages to design a better bridge for the railroad.

## Analysis:

Everywhere she has been looking lately, when she sees something new and well-made it has the stamp of a company in Colorado on it. The only people who will back her new rail line are those men who own successful businesses in CO and need her rail to sell their products.

The Washington man for Rearden is obviously playing for the other side, as is clear now. Orren Boyle has been in Washington for weeks to get this bill slipped through – it was announced publically and the vote taken all in 45 minutes! The final push came when Hank would not sell the rights to his new metal to a representative from the State Science Institute who wanted to buy it so they could NOT produce the metal.

## Key Takeaways:

We hear minor characters saying, "Who is John Galt?" This is why Dagny defiantly decided to use it as the name of her new rail line. She told Francisco this when she was begging him for money. While he refused, we see it pained him to do this and he was shocked then amused at the name. He also mysteriously warned her that John Galt may come to claim that rail line.

A little more legend is given about John Galt – this one is that he was looking for the fountain of youth. He looked for years, then spent ten years climbing to a mountain top and found it. He wanted to bring it back to all of mankind but found that it could not be brought down – a bum told this version to Dagny in a coffee shop.

Ms. Rand uses the once grand, now tired Dr. Robert Stadler to get across the idea that continuously fighting against the looters can wear a good person down:

> He came closer; he leaned with one hand against the wall above her head, almost as if he wished to hold her in the circle of his arm. "Miss Taggart," he said, a tone of gentle, bitter persuasiveness in his voice, "I am older than you. Believe me, there is no other way to live on earth. Men are not

open to truth or reason. They cannot be reached by a rational argument. The mind is powerless against them. Yet we have to deal with them. If we want to accomplish anything, we have to deceive them into letting us accomplish it. Or force them. They understand nothing else. We cannot expect their support for any endeavor of the intellect, for any goal of the spirit. They are nothing but vicious animals. They are greedy, self-indulgent, predatory ..."

# Part 1:
# Chapter 8 – THE JOHN GALT LINE

## What Happens?

Eddie Willers is having dinner in the basement cafeteria with that mysterious worker, even though others feel that, in his position as acting Vice-President, this is not appropriate. The worker slips in questions about Dagny and also learns about the contracts she is making to keep the John Galt line running – specifically Dwight Sanders who is to provide her with diesel engines. Dagny is working in a cramped office off an alley now, kicked out of her larger office by her brother while this scheme plays out. She notices the shadow of a man pacing back and forth in front of her door after midnight – he can't decide if he wants to leave or come to speak with her. Finally he fades away.

The day of the first run on the John Galt line arrives. The papers are all full of predictions that the new metal bridge will fail. Dagny and Rearden ride in the engine as it speeds at 100 mph along the track toward Colorado. They are excited and proud and, as they stand near each other, they realize they are both attracted to each other. The run is successful! The night ends with Rearden and Dagny becoming lovers.

## Analysis:

More businesses are going bankrupt. Suddenly Dwight Sanders retires and there is not a trace of him to be found after he settles his business. Now who is going to supply the engines for future business on the John Galt line?

The joy of accomplishment is stressed in the blindingly fast train ride and the fact that the older workers and the very young all are excited at the success of the line. It is also expressed in the love scene between Rearden and Dagny. It seems like the good guys may have won this round.

## Key Takeaways:

The Equalization of Opportunity Bill is forcing owners to sell off portions of their businesses so they only own one type of business. The government is funding the buy up of the extras; Paul Larkin, who has now been seen with the looter crowd, buys some. Wesley Mouch retires form Rearden Steel and is now appointed Assistant Coordinator of the Bureau of Economic Planning and National Resources. There can be no doubt that this is now a coordinated effort to seize all well-running businesses.

# Part 1:
# Chapter 9 – THE SACRED AND THE PROFANE

## What Happens?

Rearden feels guilt and announces to Dagny that he feels like an animal and is shocked she is an animal too. He claims he will never love her, but will give up everything he has to stay her lover. She laughs at him with delight and claims the same thing. He is confused and she is joyous as they begin their affair. Rearden begins a habit of dropping in at her apartment unannounced whenever he feels like it, using a key she gave him.

James is plotting with his board to buy the John Galt line back from Dagny, realizing he is being sly and feels terrible, yet can't stop his looting plans. Meanwhile, Ragnar has just seized another ship full of emergency "gifts." They seem connected in James' thoughts.

Rearden and Dagny take a vacation, driving around the country, seeing houses that aren't being maintained and painted, things still falling apart. As she can't get her diesel engines built, she wants to visit a closed motor plant – Twentieth Century Motor Company. What use is a railroad if there are no engines to pull the trains? They found 20th Century and it was rusted and empty except for a coil of wires in an old lab. It was part of an experimental new motor! The manual for it was missing parts but the idea was to draw static electricity from the air to power the motor. Free Energy!

## Analysis:

Ms. Rand uses a young girl, Cherryl Brooks, to play off of James in a scene in which he picks her up because she had read about him in the papers – the papers are saying *he* did everything Dagny did and he is taking all the credit. Cherryl, in her admiration, is used to point out to James all his failings and how his sister has been the strong one all along. Dagny has had to sign the John Galt line back to TT and James' control. It is now the Rio Norte Line again.

To make that coil motor work, they need to find the inventor. The need for intelligent men is stressed again. Without these men the world will sink backwards. Dagny ends the chapter by looking out on poor houses lit only by candles.

## Key Takeaways:

The strength of the builders is now the only thing moving the economy forward. Through the efforts of Dagny and Rearden, others (like Cherryl) still have hope. "That future that they're all talking and trembling about – it will be as you made it, because you had the courage none of them could conceive of. All the roads to wealth that they're scrambling for now, it's your strength that broke them open. The strength to stand against everyone. The strength to recognize no will but your own."

The move toward CO continues – companies from CT, MA and NJ are all closing up and moving to CO. It is blamed on the Equalization of Opportunity Bill: since every business owner must now make a choice as to the only business they will own, they are choosing the ones doing the best and they all seem to be in CO.

The looters wonder why things are staying the same for them. They wonder why these business owners are choosing to go to CO where the government is small and only deals with the courts and police. They cry it isn't right: "Well, things are being done," he said. "Steps are being taken. Constructive steps. The Legislature has passed a Bill giving wider powers to the Bureau of Economic Planning and National Resources. They've appointed a very able man as Top Coordinator. Can't say I've heard of him before, but the newspapers said he's a man to be watched. His name is Wesley Mouch."

# Part 1:
# Chapter 10 – WYATT'S TORCH

## What Happens?

Dagny and Rearden try to find out who owns 20th Century so they can try to track down the person who created the coil motor. It was sold twice at the same time, so it is all tied up in court. When she calls NYC to get Eddie to send TT engineers to the factory to see if they can gather more parts and information, Eddie is in a panic and informs her "they" are trying to kill CO.

Dagny ignores harsh new regulations that are being passed in Washington to go on a hunt to find anyone who knows anything about the coil motor. She follows many dead ends and finally only comes up with the three Starnes heirs of the original owner, Jeb Starnes. All three children are spoiled and not able to work. One does remember the name of William Hastings and that he left for Wyoming. She tracks him down and finds he died five years ago; however, his wife says he did not invent the motor, his twenty-six-year-old assistant did and she can't recall the name. She gives Dagny a lead: there is a cook at a little place in the mountains who was a friend of her husband and the young inventor, though she remembers no names.

## Analysis:

The new push from the looters is to enact a flurry of new laws, which will drag down the producers all to the lowest common denominator: no trains can go faster than the junky trains; no company can produce more than the one losing money; and the best of the worst is that no business is allowed to move out of the state they are in now. *All in the name of freedom.* Ellis Wyatt swore before to take them all down with him if they ruined his business – will he?

Dagny tries to make her brother see that if the good producers are all killed, it will benefit the looters only for a short period of time; then, with nothing new, they will all be living in caves. Rearden contrasts his unspoken love for Dagny, which is selfless, to Lillian wanting him to sacrifice to fake a love for her. To her, the sacrifice is all she wants – not true love.

The story of another person who has disappeared comes to Dagny: Midas Mulligan, a rich banker, disappeared seven years ago. The last person to see him sold him bluebells (flowers) and he was smiling, saying how glad he was to be alive. Judge Narragansett had also disappeared – one of the best judges.

Another big hint provided to us readers is spoken to Dagny by the cook: "There is only one helpful suggestion that I can give you: By the essence and nature of existence, contradictions cannot exist. If you find it inconceivable that an invention of genius should be abandoned among ruins, and that a philosopher should wish to work as a cook in a diner – check your premises. You will find that one of them is wrong." She started: she remembered that she had heard this before and that it was Francisco who had said it. And then she remembered that this man had been one of Francisco's teachers.

## Key Takeaways:

Eugene Lawson is saying to Dagny the same things all the looters say: he can't be held responsible for the collapse of the bank he was president of. Like always, he babbles on and she repeats the simple question, trying to find the name of the motor's engineer. She doesn't care about blame – yet he goes on defending himself, despite the fact he hasn't even been attacked, just as so many have done in each chapter. It is because they feel their own guilt. He echoed that he never made a profit. It disgusts Dagny to hear this.

The falseness of pity is addressed again: "Why yes, I can," said Midas Mulligan when he was asked whether he could name a person more evil than the man with a heart closed to pity. "The man who uses another's pity for him as a weapon."

Good work is appreciated by others who do good work. Dagny can even recognize a well-made hamburger over one thrown together. The sight of a well-kept house even with only basic furniture is noticed as superior by Dagny over one with expensive items that are not appreciated or cared for properly. A sloppy mind spills over, making a sloppy life.

The chapter ends with Wyatt blowing up his oil fields and disappearing. A note says, "I am leaving it as I found it. Take over. It's yours."

# PART TWO:

## EITHER-OR

# Part 2:
# Chapter 1 – THE MAN WHO BELONGED ON EARTH

## What Happens?

Dr. Stadler's assistant, Dr. Floyd Ferris, just back from Washington, had published a book of nonsense under the name of the State Science Institute – which basically went on and on like: "Do not expect consistency. Everything is a contradiction of everything else. Nothing exists but contradictions... Do not look for 'common sense.' To demand 'sense' is the hallmark of nonsense." Also, Dr. Ferris is trying to hide something called Project X. Rearden received an order for 10,000 tons of Rearden metal for Project X and refused to send it.

Dagny is meeting with Dr. Stadler to see if he knows the engineer who created the motor. Meanwhile she is crossing off runs on her train schedule as businesses shut down. He knows of a student, Quentin Daniels, who may be able to work on the motor and figure it out. They overhear workers saying, "Who is John Galt?" and he says he knew a John Galt, but thinks he is dead.

## Analysis:

Businesses are closing down like dominoes in CO now that Wyatt has left; in turn, this is affecting the entire nation with shortages. People have to apply to Washington pleading "special need" in order to get supplies and it seems that only people who have friends in Washington get approved. Rearden now has no control over who buys his new metal.

Rearden is starting to see that he is not an animal for wanting Dagny, but that it is an expression of his own joy; the joy of being alive and having something of value.

## Key Takeaways:

When good men do nothing, the evil men gain power. When good men are in the company of great men, they feel safer, happier.

Both Dagny and Rearden are close to understanding a little more about their view of the world, but they are not quite there: he about his sexual desire and she about the purpose of her work. They both wonder that if there are other good people out there then they shouldn't give up fighting to make the world a better place. They realize that the looters seem afraid when they don't go along with their ridiculous plans; there is something about the looters' motive that they are missing.

# Part 2:
# Chapter 2 – THE ARISTOCRACY OF PULL

## What Happens?

Nearly all the businesses in CO are now closed – the good people disappeared. They promise they would never leave but they do – and with no note or letter.

Dagny has to attend Jim's wedding. She has never even met the fiancée, Cherryl. Rearden is meeting clients and suppliers he wants to deal with secretly in his hotel room, knowing he could be imprisoned if the government found out. They decide if an employee finds out, they will pay the blackmail; if anyone with a government connection finds out, they will not pay and will go to jail. Lillian surprises him and bursts into his hotel room demanding that they go to Jim's wedding.

## Analysis:

Dagny has the premise that there is a destroyer moving through the country. She thinks she is running a race against whatever is happening to the good people who are disappearing.

James is holding up Cherryl as a weapon against the looters and his sister, as some form of defiance because his life is eating him alive. So he decides to marry the poorest *honest* girl he knows – still fooling her into thinking he is one of the good guys. Orren Boyle (mill owner) and Bertram Scudder (journalist) are at the wedding and have been peppered throughout the chapters, always lurking and always ready to warp things to their advantage using people's fear or collected favors for later, never being straight up. Orren says to Jim that he can pay for a man in Washington, but he feels better when he has something over his man, then he knows no one can pay him more. Blackmail. Francisco shows up at the wedding and we find out he knows that James is a large stockholder in d'Anconia Copper. We find that most of the people that profited from the robbing of Rearden Steel have invested out of country in d'Anconia Copper. (Sounds like the issues of today.)

Francisco gives a long speech about the history, power and making of money. It is not evil, but having it without earning it is. He sings the praises of the American Industrialist. Rearden is there and knows he was talking about him and men like him.

## Key Takeaways:

Lillian finally shows some of the "pull" she is working on: she lets James know that he now owes her a favor for bringing her husband to the wedding and allowing the others to think that James had some kind of control over Hank. It is shown that the looters have no internal friendship, only ties of money and blackmail and fear. "We will liberate our culture from the stranglehold of the profit-chasers. We will build a society dedicated to higher ideals, and we will replace the aristocracy of money by – Francisco finishes the sentence – the aristocracy of pull."

# Part 2:
# Chapter 3 – WHITE BLACKMAIL

## What Happens?

Hank drops Lillian off at a train and spends the night at Dagny's. When he returns to his hotel in the morning he is surprised by Lillian waiting over breakfast for him. She refuses to give him a divorce, telling him she will take pleasure in being there to remind him he is not perfect and didn't keep his word to her.

Dr. Ferris visits Rearden and tries to blackmail him into delivering the new metal for Project X or he will expose that he knows Rearden was selling it illegally to Danagger. Rearden says he looks forward to the public trial.

Eddies talks to the mysterious worker again, mentioning that Dagny is sure there is a man behind the destroyer and she wants to get to the good men before the destroyer does. He mentions that she is on her way to Pittsburgh to try to keep Danagger from disappearing. When Dagny reaches him, someone is already in his office. She is too late; he is going to retire that night.

Late at night an alarm goes off at the steel mill. Rearden and Francisco race to the furnace where streaks of molten metal were running all over the floor. In the midst of jets of burning steam, Francisco and Rearden stand side by side and manually dam up the hole in the furnace and save the workers.

## Analysis:

It is stressed again how Rearden and many of the good ones left take on the burden of others, or say the others *are* not doing this on purpose. Yet something in their sly manner hints that they are doing this to be cruel. Rearden is still trying to push that thought out of his mind.

Dagny is still refusing to break down the things she thinks do not make sense. If Danagger loves Rearden and loves industry, how can he leave? She is not digging deep enough, yet hints are all around her now and she knows no one is being killed or kidnapped, because Danagger is very calm and happy about his retirement. Francisco talks to Rearden about why he accepts being punished for inventing his metal – would he just turn his whole factory over to the looters? Rearden growls that he would blow it up first. "Then why don't you do it, Mr. Rearden?" Rearden is realizing he is placing his virtue in the service of evil when he thought he was doing good. Here is where Ms. Rand connects to Atlas holding the world on his shoulders – a world getting heavier in response to the more Atlas tries. *Francisco would tell Atlas to shrug!*

## Key Takeaways:

Hank tries to get Dagny to name her first lover. She won't. She pushes to understand that he wants to know this because he has not yet fully accepted that he is worthy of her wanting him and therefore may be trying to compare himself to a worse or better man. Hank is still struggling with having sexual feelings and not considering them disgusting – but he is starting to understand how it can be joyous and not bad (a sin).

The new laws: Dr. Ferris lets slip when he is trying to blackmail Rearden that he doesn't care that the law was broken, only that this gives him leverage to blackmail Rearden into doing favors for him. One more hint that the looters are not innocent: "The only power any government has is the power to crack down on criminals. Well, when there aren't enough criminals, one makes them. One declares so many things to be a crime that it becomes impossible for men to live without breaking laws."

Foreshadowing: Danagger says to Dagny he won't say goodbye; she will be joining him someday.

# Part 2:
# Chapter 4 – THE SANCTION OF THE VICTIM

## What Happens?

Over Thanksgiving dinner, Rearden's mother, brother and wife tell him he should find someone to fix the trial and yell at him about his believing he is so perfect. Lillian was trying to use guilt by hinting at his cheating on her. But he can't feel guilty because he doesn't care about her now – the same with any verdict from the trial.

TT rail is falling apart. Dagny can't get enough new metal to repair it, only patch parts. Rearden is at the TT offices on Thanksgiving night, so is Eddie. Rearden sets up a deal to deliver all the new metal Dagny needs and to muddle the paperwork so no one can put her on trial.

At his trial, Rearden says to his judge, "I have no defense... I do not recognize this court's right to try me." He gives a long speech about hard work and fair exchange. At the end, the audience erupts in applause. The judges are afraid because they know no one else can keep the metal in production. They sentence him to a 5K fine and then suspend the sentence. Since Rearden didn't play along with them voluntarily, they failed in trying to bully him.

## Analysis:

Rearden realized Lillian is happier now that she can hold his cheating over him, though he still can't say it completely and then look at her as evil yet. In addition, when Philip says he thinks Hank should go to jail and Rearden quietly says that if he says that again he will be kicked out of the house with only the change in his pockets. He realized that they all knew they were at his mercy before he did. He realizes that he doesn't have to be part of their standards. He leaves for NYC against his wife's wishes.

Another link in Rearden's thought process is that he is sorry that by saving himself he will be saving others who don't deserve it. The next link comes from a talk with Francisco where he talks about the person one chooses as a sex partner reflecting what a person really thinks of themselves. Rearden's eyes are opening to a new way to look at desire. In this talk, the reader comes to know that Francisco still loves Dagny. Rearden doesn't know the woman Francisco is talking about is also the woman he loves. Francisco says he hopes he has not lost her love for all time. We now see the paths of our heroes may clash on this point in the future.

## Key Takeaways:

Rearden sees the "Intensity of contemplating a vision with a bitter wonder that was almost fear. He was seeing the enormity of the smallness of the enemy who was destroying the world." Dagny has taken heart from the trial and it has given her energy to "Fight on."

Another hint: when Rearden revels he has ordered copper from d'Anconia copper, Francisco is in despair – reminding him that he had said never to do business with his companies. He refuses to tell Rearden why, telling him the same thing he asked Dagny years ago – when you hate me, please believe me that I am your friend. Rearden loses a bundle of money when Ragnar attacks and sinks the ships carrying the copper order.

# Part 2:
# Chapter 5 – ACCOUNT OVERDRAWN

## What Happens?

Now the rest of the world is closing down like CO did. England is crying that they are starving – and relief ships sent with aid are seized by the pirate Ragnar Danneskjöld. TT trains are breaking down. There are no new supplies anywhere; once something breaks, that is the end of that task – be it snowplowing or building homes. Even Rearden can't deliver on his orders because he can't get copper. Tracks are falling apart and people are now starting to die in the wrecks.

At a TT Board meeting, Weatherby, a government man, is putting pressure on James and TT to raise wages and reduce the number of trains running. It looks like James is losing his influence in Washington and he is now a target instead of one of the gang. The board decides to rip up the John Galt line and use the rails on the main track.

Lillian shows up unexpectedly to catch Rearden with his mistress and is shocked to find out it is Dagny. She says to him, "Anyone but her." She demands he give her up, screaming that she owns him and has first claim on him. She won't say why the fact that it is Dagny infuriates her. He says he would like a divorce but that if Lillian still wants the marriage, he will not push her. She will stay married in the hope of still having influence over him.

## Analysis:

Francisco is waiting for Dagny after the news of the John Galt line. He was there for her worst moment. He tells her of his ancestor who waited fifteen years for the woman he loved, not knowing if she would wait for him because she could not live through the battle he fought to re-establish his empire. Dagny gets the hint, wondering if he ever wanted to marry her. Thinking it may be a trap, she says nothing. As they leave, he gives another hint: "John Galt is Prometheus who changed his mind. After centuries of being torn by vultures in payment for having brought to men the fire of the gods, he broke his chains – and he withdrew his fire – until the day when men withdraw their vultures."

## Key Takeaways:

Ragnar is taking as many relief ships as he can. He puts the crew off in life boats and takes the whole ship – but he never takes the ships with d'Anconia copper – he always sinks those ships.

The contract between loveless sex and lovemaking is stressed as Rearden thinks about his cold wife in comparison to Dagny, who cares for him. His disgust for needing sex is now completely gone – he understands how precious it is to share desire and love at once.

# Part 2:
# Chapter 6 – MIRACLE METAL

## What Happens?

Mouch invites all the looters to Washington in connection with the national crisis: James, Orren Boyle, Dr. Ferris, Mr. Weatherby, Eugene Lawson and a new player, Mr. Thompson. They go forward with **Directive 10-289** ... saying freedom has failed because each year is getting worse; they will get the backing of the press and declare a national emergency. Now no workers can leave or change jobs and they cannot be fired – same with business owners. All patents and copyrights are to be turned over to the government. No new inventions are permitted. Everyone must – by law – produce the same amount this year as they produced last year, and everyone must spend the same amount of money as they did last year. Francisco called it **the Moratorium on Brains**.

Dagny resigns and heads out to the country until she can get her head around what has just happened.

## Analysis:

With nothing new being made, the looters have less and they start to fight among themselves. They are still trying to control everything as a group, but we can see now that they will each sell out the other to be the last to starve to death. With Directive 10-289, they are also trying to stop the good people from disappearing. They realize that civilization has to have people who work and make things.

Lillian has shared the information about her husband's affair with the looters. They blackmail him and threaten that if he doesn't go along with them, they will make it all public. It won't really hurt him, but it will hurt Dagny's reputation – dragging her through the mud and putting her on display. (Remember this is when there was very little divorce and most women didn't even work – this would have been a huge scandal – stirring up disgust; bigger than Kanye West "dissing" Taylor Swift at the awards show – bigger than anything that would hit and disappear today. Back then, a scandal would hang with you for decades, not just months.)

## Key Takeaways:

James Taggart brags to his group that he can make Rearden sign off on the Directive. As they set the date for the law to go into effect, James pulls the curtain to shut off his view of the Washington Monument.

The Gift Certificate: the name given to the document that they want owners/inventors to sign to give all rights over to the government, thinking the false words will fool the general public and make it look like a voluntary action on the part of the people being robbed.

# Part 2:
# Chapter 7 – THE MORATORIUM ON BRAINS

## What Happens?

Eddie is talking to the mysterious worker again. Workers are quitting because they resent being chained to their jobs. People are wandering the streets but the jail has no food or room, so they are not being arrested for quitting. As Eddie babbles, he inadvertently gives away enough information that the worker now knows exactly where Dagny's cabin is.

Rearden moves out of his big house, leaving it to his mother, brother and Lillian. Hank files for divorce – telling his attorney to frame her if need be but to make sure she gets no property or alimony.

Rearden runs into Ragnar on a midnight walk home. Ragnar has been putting the money he makes selling his plunder into Mulligan Bank, into accounts that match the income tax that people such as Rearden have paid – in accounts in their names. Rearden says that the Mulligan Bank in Chicago has closed. Ragnar only says that the bank is not in Chicago. Ragnar says he will blow up any factory that tries to produce Rearden metal and the people will think there is a curse on it. Then Ragnar gives him a gold bar, saying it is a payment. Though Rearden says he will turn the pirate in, when a cop car cruises past, Rearden says Ragnar is his new bodyguard and had been ready to shoot the cops if they made any move. Ragnar then disappears into the night.

## Analysis:

A train carrying a Washington man, Kip, derails on the way to a rally. The problems are all issues that competent workers had let their bosses know about, but the bosses had all made decisions that fulfilled favors they had promised. The looters are ruining themselves and won't admit it – what they do is say that they had better make all railroads property of the government so this doesn't happen again. Still refusing to see facts and reason, Kip demands that they not wait for a diesel engine to go through the tunnel, but use the old coal-burning one. Rail works say it is not safe. Kip says he will have them fired if they do not get him moving. Men of principle quit, bums and drunkards just on the job send the train into the tunnel. It never makes it out – all passengers died in the tunnel.

## Key Takeaways:

Human Ability: Ragar says he is not loved by the world, not recognized, but he loves human ability and that is why he is risking his life. He is bringing justice to those stealing the products of human ability.

# Part 2:
# Chapter 8 – BY OUR LOVE

## What Happens?

Dagny is gardening at her cabin, trying to forget the railroad and the insanity. She has waited for Rearden to come to her for weeks now. A car rolls up but it is Francisco who gets out, not Hank. "Hi, Slug!" "Hi, Frisco!" Then he suddenly kisses her. She knows now that he loves her, but can't erase the thought of him selling out and become a playboy looter. He asks her if she could have stood the torture of the last month twelve years ago. She says, "No." He smiles then says, "I am ready to tell you everything now." He starts to tell her how he did it all on purpose to leave nothing to the looters; that they can rebuild, but the looters can't. Before he can finish, they hear a radio broadcast: the Comet passengers were suffocating to death in the tunnel. A series of miscommunications didn't signal the Army Special to wait, and the two trains had crashed inside the tunnel. All were lost but one man to tell the story.

Dagny rushes to her car, leaving Francisco screaming for her not to go back.

## Analysis:

Francisco is whistling Halley's Fifth Concerto as he walks up to Dagny. He now has nothing to hide. Before he can reveal all he has to tell her, Dagny is back at TT – trying to get the trains running again and clean up after the Comet disaster. She tells Mouch in Washington that she will be breaking laws to get things running again. She is told she has an old-fashioned view of laws; that laws change now according to circumstances and the people involved. Washington wants her to get the rails running again. James is falling apart, trying to place the blame on anyone but himself.

## Key Takeaways:

Dagny and Rearden say they will keep on working as long as they can – even though they now know that they are being used; that because they love their work, it is being held ransom so their efforts can be grabbed by the government as soon as they are finished.

# Part 2:
# Chapter 9 – THE FACE WITHOUT PAIN OR FEAR OR GUILT

## What Happens?

Francisco visits Dagny. When she declares she will work until she is dead in order to keep the rail running, he declares that they are now enemies; that she doesn't understand that she almost walked into heaven and ran back to earth. Since she now knows that the looters have no honor and are doing all this purposely – he is out to ruin her efforts so the looters can't use it. She says if she is wrong she may have to beg him on her knees for forgiveness. He implies that sex would be his choice. She knows it is killing him to do this. She asks him how he can do it. He says it is his love for her and the good men of the world.

Using his key, Rearden walks in on them as they are having this passionate conversation. He starts to tell Frisco to stay away; that he is not good enough for Dagny, when it hits him that *SHE* is the only woman Frisco ever loved. Rearden hits him. Frisco shows his greatest love for both Dagny and Rearden by not fighting back and leaves.

## Analysis:

With more hints given, Francisco tells Dagny she has to take the road herself – to Atlantis, the city only heroes can enter. He lets her know he is waiting for a Second Renaissance as soon as she is finished helping the looters destroy the world. He says he will wait for her (like he said when they were kids).

Giving up the fight to make the world a better place feels like failure to her. Quentin tells Dagny in a letter that he will no longer work on the coil motor. He ends his letter: "It is a strange feeling – writing this letter. I do not intend to die, but I am giving up the world and this feels like the letter of a suicide. So I want to say that of all the people I have known, you are the only person I regret leaving behind. Sincerely yours, Quentin Daniels."

## Key Takeaways:

Eddie ends the chapter realizing, as he helps her pack, that Dagny is sleeping with Hank. He keeps it from her, but now realizes that he is in love with her too. In his despair he goes to talk with the mysterious worker, speaking to him like a priest – unloading all his cares. Not only does he talk about her love life, but also lets slip that Dagny is trying to reach Quentin before the destroyer does, to try to keep him from disappearing. Suddenly the mysterious worker has to leave.

# Part 2:
# Chapter 10 – THE SIGN OF THE DOLLAR

## What Happens?

Dagny streaks West to try to save Quentin. On her train she runs into a bum who is about to be kicked off. She sees he has a little dignity in a clean collar and patched holes. She has him to dinner and learns he worked at the 20th Century Motor Company; he was there when the Starnes heirs starting paying people according to what they needed and working people according to how long they could stand it. Soon everyone was hiding any strength or potential they had. They had to vote on the salaries paid out. They began to hate each other and to cheat and lie just to get a decent wage.

Dagny wakes up in her train car – the train has stopped dead on the track and the crew has just left it there and disappeared. She is happy for them, then realizes what that means. She starts to work to get a new crew to her train. The rest of the passengers are just sitting around like sheep. Owen Kellogg is a passenger on her train (chapter one – worker who refused a promotion) and offers to walk with her to a call box. They have to walk twenty miles before they reach one that works. Dagny flies an abandoned plane by herself to continue her journey.

As she lands the plane, another is taking off. Dagny learns that Quentin has just left in that plane! Some man had come for him a few hours before. She rushes back into her plane to chase them down!

They are flying into a storm over the CO mountains. She is chasing an unknown airplane to save the motor, save the world – and is ready to fight the pilot to the death to get Quentin back.

## Analysis:

The slogan, "From each according to his ability, to each according to his need" – this is the basic premise of the Marxist Socialism that fueled the Cold War. Using the 20th Century factory, showing how it could all really pan out if left to run its course.

Even Dagny is not immune to cursing ... as she follows the other airplane, it looks as if it has flown straight into the mountain – but there is no wreckage. As she circles looking for survivors, she sees she is dangerously low on fuel; she is closer to the valley than she thought. Her motor stops, she tries to glide in for a landing and crashes in the valley. She curses: "Oh, hell! Who is John Galt?"

## Key Takeaways:

FINALLY we know; in a meeting at the 20th Century factory, when the owners were telling the 6,000 employees that they couldn't quit and that they all belonged to each other, one young engineer stood up and said, "I don't." He was laughed at when he said he was going to put an end to all of this. When asked *how*; he said, "I will stop the motor of the world." Then he walked out. *His name was John Galt.*

# PART THREE:

## A IS A

# Part 3:
# Chapter 1 – ATLANTIS

## What Happens?

Dagny wakes up looking into John Galt's eyes. He was the pilot she was following. She feels at peace, but she is hurt. John carries her along as she asks how she got here – she was circling a mountain then dropped right into a valley. He has her look up – she sees shimmering air. Refractor rays to hide the valley! (This is the first use of this idea that I have come across – so imagine how cool it was to read for the first time.)

Galt takes her on a tour of the valley. There are many men and a few women. They have their own mint – making their own one- and five-dollar coins with the Statue of Liberty on one side – smaller than pennies and of pure gold. She is shown Frisco's house, a modest log cabin with his family coat of arms over the door. Galt says this was the first person he took away from her. As he drives her and carries her around, they both notice an attraction for each other.

## Analysis:

Ms. Rand shows us this paradise where all the good men have gone. John Galt, the engineer who created the coil motor, is the town's handyman. A judge makes butter and handles legal affairs. Dwight Sanders makes their new airplanes and has a farm. And so on for all the cool people that left Dagny's world. They all pay for everything with pure gold. The trend is that everyone does more than one job: one that they use their mind for and one that produces necessities. The author is emphasizing that there is no "lousy job – only lousy men who don't care to do it." They are not looters; they do not think that one man's ability is a threat to another's. If a better worker puts them out of their job, then they are glad to work for that better man or find a new job.

Should heaven wait for our dreams when we are dead, or should we live it now? This is basically what all the men are asking Dagny at a dinner. Galt tells Dagny to check her premises again when she tries to get them to share their new inventions and the coil motor with the world – "None of us has given up. It is the world that has ... We are on strike." Men of intelligence are on strike and Galt started it all. They ask her if she is ready to see TT crumble to dust and start over here, with them. She is not ready to give them an answer. She still feels like she is a coward or running away. They say they will only return when the rest of the world gives up the code of the looters – but it looks like it may happen soon as so much is crumbling. They say they will come back and rebuild the world when they can do it under their own values and not as slaves.

## Key Takeaways:

John Galt's Motto cut in granite over the entrance to the power station that runs the whole valley:

> I SWEAR BY MY LIFE AND MY LOVE OF IT THAT I WILL NEVER LIVE FOR THE SAKE OF ANOTHER MAN, NOR ASK ANOTHER MAN TO LIVE FOR MINE.

# Part 3:
# Chapter 2 – THE UTOPIA OF GREED

## What Happens?

Dagny wakes up to Ragnar watching her. He, John and Frisco have had breakfast together every June 1st for twelve years; however, Frisco has not shown up yet. When Owen Kellogg shows up, he reports that the world thinks Dagny has crashed and died. Dagny wants to leave, but according to the rules, everyone here has to stay for a month. They all stay for that one month of vacation and no one leaves. Some live there full time; some come only for that one month. She can't even get a message out to Rearden so he will know she is alive. She is heartbroken because she knows he is searching for her plane wreck. She works as Galt's housekeeper, to earn her keep because she doesn't want to be a moocher in this valley.

Francisco finally arrives. He was late because of her "death." When he sees her there, he falls on his knees in front of her. He tells her he accepts her love for Rearden and still loves her but is only grateful she is alive and will not stand in her way. She, however, now wants Galt and has no idea if that will work or not, yet she still loves Frisco and Hank. She has no idea how to process all of this, or of the best way to handle this issue.

Dagny gets a personal performance of the Fifth Concerto and enjoys more of the peace of the valley. Dr. Akston invites his three pupils to dinner: John, Frisco and Ragnar; plus Ragnar's wife, Kay Ludlow, and Dagny. This now answers that mystery of the students. They talk philosophy and how they all met in college. They mention Dr. Stadler, but say he is lost to weakness and bitterness.

## Analysis:

Dagny is still feeling that she will have to give up paradise or give up the world – she is still looking at it as an either/or situation. She also realizes she very much wants to live with and be a part of John Galt. To do so, she will have to be one hundred percent convinced to leave the world to the looters. She is in torment.

Dagny's love for the Taggart Bridge is what makes up her mind to go back into the world. The thought of it being blown up is too much for her to take. The men let her go on the condition she not tell anyone about them or the valley. They are not angry with her; they know she is doing it because she loves human achievement.

## Key Takeaways:

Patriotism: "This country was the only country in history born, not of chance and blind tribal warfare, but as a rational product of man's mind." They plan to rebuild the United States when the time is right.

Evil: One must know what good is before you can name evil. Everyone has the power to choose – if they don't use that power then they sink into chaos and that is a choice too.

Desire: In the valley, one must not be fake. Illustrated with falling in love, if you desire someone you have to be honest with yourself and them – even if more than the two are involved, as no one can be responsible for another's happiness. In addition, if following honesty and ability and merit, then there is no conflict of interests; omit the irrational from one's outlook and don't call for anyone to sacrifice and then no one is a threat to another.

Example: when Frisco finds out that Galt loves Dagny, he is shocked for a second and then says, of course, a man like you would love her too – and accepts that his chance is over. The three stay friends.

# Part 3:
# Chapter 3 – ANTI-GREED

## What Happens?

Dr. Stadler is pushed into a ceremony and press release when he has no idea what is going on. Dr. Ferris and Mr. Thompson have set him up with the press to talk about Project X and he doesn't even know what it is – so all he says are general sound bites and the press eats it up. Dr. Ferris now talks to the huge crowed – it is the Thompson Harmonizer, a weapon of sound vibrations. While Ferris is blathering on about hard work, Dr. Stadler watches some goats tied out on a nearby deserted farm. A baby goat is frolicking around its mother. The machine is turned on and there is grisly destruction. "There is no nail or rivet remaining in the frame of the structure and there is no blood vessel left unbroken in the bodies of the animals," they say proudly. Dr. Ferris says no enemy would attack them now – the country is now free from fear and aggression. The crowd is disturbed, but says nothing.

Dagny returns to find Mr. Meigs, the Washington rep of the **Railroad Unification Plan**, in her office giving orders so that friends of Washington will get their grapefruits. James is in a state of panic every day now. He barely welcomes Dagny back to the land of the living before he shoves her at Mr. Meigs.

Jim wants her to go on the radio, Bertram Scudder's program, and assure the public that she didn't quit. She refuses. Oddly, Lillian Rearden steps in and tells her she will do the show. Lillian says Dagny doing this will have the same effect as when Rearden signed the Gift Certificate. Lillian goes on to tell her Rearden did it to save her reputation and honor. Lillian proudly states that she was the one who took his metal away from him and gave the information to the government. She threatens Dagny the same way.

Dagny agrees to go on the show, but she fools them and says over the air not only that she had an affair with him, but that they blackmailed him and that was the only reason he signed the Gift Certificate. The show goes off the air with Dagny laughing. Inside she is afraid this will kill the love Galt has for her, but she is no longer willing to lie or be fake.

Dagny returns home and Rearden is there. He nods that he heard the broadcast and is not angry with her. Dagny has the first breakdown of her life, sobbing against Hank. Then he tells her how much he loves her.

## Analysis:

Ms. Rand here clears up the issue of three men that Dagny has loved. As Rearden tells her how much he totally loves her, he says he did not say that at their beginning, but wanted to make sure he said it at their ending. She is shocked. He goes on: "Now I'll tell you what it was that you wanted to tell me – because, you see, I know it and I accept: somewhere within the past month, you have met the man you love, and if love means one's final, irreplaceable choice, then he is the only man you've ever loved." "Yes!" Her voice was half-gasp, half-scream, as if under a physical blow, the shock her only awareness. "Hank! – how did you know it?" He smiled and pointed at the radio. "My darling, you used nothing but the past tense." "I knew what you felt for me, I knew how much it was, but I knew that I was not your final choice. What you'll give him is not taken away from me, it's what I've never had. I can't rebel against it. What I've had means too much to me – and that I've had it, can never be changed."

## Key Takeaways:

"People think that a liar gains a victory over his victim. What I've learned is that a lie is an act of self-abdication, because one surrenders one's reality to the person to whom one lies, making that person one's master, condemning oneself from then on to faking the sort of reality that person's view requires to be faked. And if one gains the immediate purpose of the lie, the price one pays is the destruction of that which the gain was intended to serve. The man who lies to the world is the world's slave from then on."

# Part 3:
# Chapter 4 – ANTI-LIFE

## What Happens?

James plots the takeover of d'Anconia Copper with the other looters. Then he wanders the streets of NYC in a funk and still feeling panic. He ends up at his own home and pretends he left the banquet early to have dinner with his wife, Cherryl. Cherryl is no longer in awe of James – she is now indifferent to him. After Dagny's radio show, she realized the government works through blackmail and extortion and that James is part of the group.

Dagny has no joy in her work now – she is going from disaster to disaster just keeping things limping along. She looks for glimpses of Galt and keeps her shades open because she knows he is watching her and waiting for a time when he can come to claim her, when she is ready to accept the valley. The bright spot in her day is when Cherryl visits and tells her that everything she loved about James she found out was what Dagny did.

Cherryl returns home to find that James has had an affair with Lillian – just because she is still Hank's wife for one more month. In fact they disgust each other and just did it to "hurt" Rearden one more time. James will not give Cherryl a divorce. She is so upset she paces NYC all night and then drowns herself.

## Analysis:

Bertram Scudder has his show cancelled after Dagny's appearance. He didn't schedule her, nor did he force her to do it, nor was he involved in the blackmail – but he was the scapegoat. The looters will not hesitate to kill one of their own to save the rest. James takes advantage of other looters, trying to scrabble to the top of the heap – but he knows that one wrong move and he will be ruined too. This is the real dog-eat-dog world, and he created it.

## Key Takeaways:

Love is so special that it can't just be given out like candy. It shouldn't be causeless, just because someone wants to be loved. It should be because of what they are and that you value those traits; or love is meaningless (you could then love anyone.) Love is NOT blind. Cherryl is stunned when she realizes all the looters just want to be loved, but they don't want to earn it or be worthy of it.

Justice: "Whenever anyone accuses some person of being 'unfeeling,' he means that that person is just. He means that that person has no causeless emotions and will not grant him a feeling which he does not deserve. He means that 'to feel' is to go against reason, against moral values, against reality... You never hear it said by a good person about those who fail to do him justice. But you always hear it said by a rotter about those who treat him as a rotter; those who don't feel any sympathy for the evil he's committed or for the pain he suffers as a consequence... Those who grant sympathy to guilt grant none to innocence. Ask yourself which of the two is the unfeeling person. And then you'll see what motive is the opposite of charity."

# Part 3:
# Chapter 5 – THEIR BROTHERS' KEEPERS

## What Happens?

Almost no trains are moving now. When the order comes to make d'Anconia Copper state property, all the mines are blown up. The looters who schemed to buy stock early have lost all that money. Frisco has vanished. Looters have gone from figuring the rich had years of supplies, to months, to only weeks left now. No one is thinking past getting through the upcoming winter. While the people are starving, the harvest of grain and veggies is rotting near the rail line because there are no working freight cars anymore.

A young government man who has been working at the steel mill for years and has realized he is working for looters, not brotherly love, warns Rearden that something is up. The looters are sneaking in more workers and are up to something. They don't know what the looters are planning.

Dagny discovers that Galt has been working in the tunnels for her railroad for twelve years, waiting for her. He decides that he will pay the price of loving her before she comes to the valley, and meets her in a tunnel. They finally make love. He knows that she has not decided to come to the valley yet, and he knows that if she keeps trying to save the world she may expose him to the looters. He said it was worth it to show his love. Then they part; he says not to contact him in any way until she is ready to leave this world.

## Analysis:

Dagny is at a dinner meeting with the looters. As they babble on about closing this or that rail line for the good of the rest, she realizes she is indifferent to them – she no longer looks at them as human. They are as dead to her as the phone, telegraph and signal wires that relied on copper, which no one can get now.

## Key Takeaways:

Favors: Philip finally asks his brother for a job at the steel mill. Rearden says he can't use someone like Philip. "What's more important, that your damn steel gets poured or that I eat?" "How do you propose to eat if the steel doesn't get poured?" Favors are of no use when things get down to the basics.

If man has no brain, then this is what would happen: as the train lines crumble and the wiring fails, Dagny pushes people out to hold lanterns for signaling and men to push the trains over the switch tracks. She pushes back at them that they claim there is nothing of value in thinking – so, "What did you expect?" Then she sees Galt among the men pushing trains around to get them out of the tunnel terminal.

# Part 3:
# Chapter 6 – THE CONCERTO OF DELIVERANCE

## What Happens?

Workers stage fake riots at the mill, breaking things and attacking a good foreman. Rearden realizes he feels love for his mill, but as if it is a deceased loved one: there is no action to be taken – just memories. Then the looters freeze all his bank accounts. He doesn't even fight it. He just thinks about the bar of gold given to him by a pirate.

Rearden goes to a meeting in NYC to see what the looters want next. On his drive home, he sees a mob attacking his mills. The young government boy tried to stop them and got shot. He dies in Rearden's arms, having completely come around to Rearden's side. Rearden feels murderous anger at the system that didn't allow this boy to think freely and make his own choices until it came down to life or death. As the mob dies down, Rearden is shot but pulled to safety before he is shot again. Francisco had been working in the mills for two months just to watch over Hank. Rearden is now ready to hear everything.

## Analysis:

The attack on Rearden's bank account doesn't work because he doesn't respond. The looters then try to backtrack, saying they are sorry, and whine until he agrees to meet them in Washington. They don't think they are going to get what they want from him. We find that Philip is the one who is sharing information, just like Lillian did. Now they are panicking that Rearden may be the next to disappear and are scrambling to try to keep him. Since they never understood him, they have no idea of what he might want as a form of payment, bribery or favor because his motives are so different from theirs.

## Key Takeaways:

Bargaining: The looters think they are offering Rearden a favor when they say they will let him raise the price of steel and will help him against the rioters (whom they placed in his factory), and that in turn they will create a **Steel Unification Plan**, trying to give the looted benefits to Rearden's steel mill like they did before to Orren Boyle. Rearden tells them to just take over the mill. They know they can't run it. They want to still control him, own him in fact, but pretend he has freedom. As he is refusing, James calls out, telling Rearden he will save them – he always has. Rearden realizes this was the key all along: he and Dagny had kept saving them from their own inaction. He has let it go on so long that the world is perishing – he (Rearden) is guilty. Later that night he learns that at the same time they were bargaining with him, they had also set the mob loose on his mill. He was going to lose either way.

# Part 3:
# Chapter 7 – "THIS IS JOHN GALT SPEAKING"

## What Happens?

Rearden and all the good workers at his mill have vanished. James runs to Dagny to demand she help bring Rearden back. Dagny is starting to slip into indifference once she learns that Galt went back to CO with Rearden. As the world is starving, the press is announcing Mr. Thompson will give a full report on the state of the world on November 22. Dagny is pressured to meet with him before the speech to give him her opinion. They tried to trick her into being seen by his side to imply she agreed with him. She refuses to go on camera, but they have lost control of the station anyway! They can't broadcast. Suddenly the voice of John Galt comes over the radio and he gives a very long speech about loving life and not sacrificing values. This speech is almost the whole chapter; it sums up in one chapter the philosophy of the whole book, and really should be read from start to finish.

## Analysis:

Parts of Galt's speech say it all: according to them, you have destroyed all that which you held to be evil and achieved all that which you held to be good. Why, then, do you shrink in horror from the sight of the world around you? That world is not the product of your sins; it is the product and the image of your virtues. It is your moral ideal brought into reality in its full and final perfection.

You have fought for it, you have dreamed of it, you have wished it, and I – I am the man who has granted you your wish.

Men do not live by the mind, you say? I have withdrawn those who do. The mind is impotent, you say? I have withdrawn those whose mind isn't. There are values higher than the mind, you say? I have withdrawn those for whom there aren't. "While you were dragging to your sacrificial altars the men of justice, of independence, of reason, of wealth, of self-esteem – I beat you to it...We are on strike. You have nothing to offer us ... neither life nor happiness can be achieved by the pursuit of irrational whims. Just as man is free to attempt to survive in any random manner, but will perish unless he lives as his nature requires, so he is free to seek his happiness in any mindless fraud, but the torture of frustration is all he will find, unless he seeks the happiness proper to man. The purpose of morality is to teach you, not to suffer and die, but to enjoy yourself and live.

## Key Takeaways:

Self-sacrifice: She wondered dimly why she should feel so glad that Rearden had found liberation, so certain that he was right – and yet refuse herself the same deliverance. Two sentences were beating in her mind. One was the triumphant sweep of: He's free, he's out of their reach! The other was like a prayer of dedication: There's still a chance to win, but let me be the only victim. Then Galt gives his speech. "This, in every hour and every issue, is your basic moral choice: thinking or non-thinking, existence or non-existence, A or non-A, entity or zero."

"I have no benefits to seek from human vices: from stupidity, dishonesty or fear. The only value men can offer me is the work of their mind. When I disagree with a rational man, I let reality be our final arbiter; if I am right, he will learn; if I am wrong, I will; one of us will win, but both will profit."

# Part 3:
# Chapter 8 – THE EGOIST

## What Happens?

After the speech, James cries that they don't have to believe it. Then the looters debate how to fool the public about that speech and still come out ahead. They don't know what to do. Dagny tells them they have to give up. They reject that and keep trying to find a way in which they will look good in the public eye.

Eddie realizes Galt is the mysterious worker he has been talking to for years.

The looters trick Dagny into thinking hired assassins are out for Galt and she leads them to his apartment. He knows she was followed and he is trapped. Dagny pretends to have turned him over to them because he says if they hurt her he will kill himself. Now he is "captured" but not cooperating. They take him at gunpoint to a PR conference and think he will just smile and be seen with them. They do this with the thinking that if the public see him there, they will assume he now has joined them. He waits until the camera pans to him and jerks away enough so everyone can see the gun jammed in his side and says, "Get the hell out of my way!"

## Analysis:

They still refuse to think: "You know the truth, all of you," she said, "and so do I, and so does every man who's heard John Galt! What else are you waiting for? For proof? He's given it to you. For facts? They're all around you. How many corpses do you intend to pile up before you renounce it – your guns, your power, your controls and the whole of your miserable altruistic creed? Give it up, if you want to live. Give it up, if there's anything left in your mind that's still able to want human beings to remain alive on this earth!" Yet they don't take her advice. This is when they put a tail on Dagny so that they can find Galt and force him into a bargain. They promise the public that they will get Galt and call for him to negotiate with them – certainly not getting the point! They even threaten to kill useless old people (their words) unless he cooperates.

# Part 3:
# Chapter 9 – THE GENERATOR

## What Happens?

Chaos hits when Galt says this on camera and moves away from the gun. They take him back to a holding cell. Dr. Stadler knows they are going to kill him in front of Galt to try to make Galt cooperate, since he was the only one Galt would talk to. Dr. Stadler races to take over Project X, but Meigs has already left NYC and taken control. The two men fight over control of the weapon. Meigs is drunk and has no idea what the buttons he is pushing will do, and ends up blowing the whole thing to dust including all the people in the building. The Taggart Bridge goes with it and now there is no connection across the Mississippi.

The looters take Galt to a torture chamber in NH to try to get him to become a puppet dictator. He is zapped with electricity but doesn't give in. James has a final mental breakdown and they leave Galt tied naked in the cellar for the night.

## Analysis:

The bridge was the last stand for Dagny. She now is ready for paradise.

## Key Takeaways:

The purpose of the haters was never to live – but to make sure intelligent men die!

## Part 3:
# Chapter 10 – IN THE NAME OF THE BEST WITHIN US

### What Happens?

Frisco, Rearden, Dagny and Ragnar break Galt out in a daring rescue with guns blazing. Then they take off for CO in a plane. They are followed by a squadron of planes that are going to wage war if Galt doesn't get out. Now they are all flying back to CO.

Eddie is left wandering the desert as the last train is frozen in place. Wagons and horses are moving people around now.

The intellectuals are busy planning how to build a railroad in their valley and are going about their happy lives – working but playing and resting also.

### Analysis:

As the planes fly over NYC in the middle of the night on their way to CO, the panicking people overload the electrical grid and the lights of the whole city go out beneath them. It is a symbol that the products of men still need good men to keep it all going. Weeks or months later, when in the valley and standing with Dagny, Galt finally says, "The road is cleared; we are going back to the world." And with that we know the strike of the mind is over and they will return and help rebuild the world – in their value system.

# Character List

(in order of importance and then appearance)

**John Galt:** Introduced at once by catch phrase, *"Who is John Galt?"* And this is what readers must try to figure out as they go along. The answer to this question is not revealed until two-thirds of the way into the story. Working to discover his true character is necessary for the whole book so cannot be given away here.

**Dagny Taggart:** Vice-President of Operations of Taggart Transcontinental (TT) Railroad – a capable, intelligent woman who struggles to save her railroad as the economy crumbles. She is in every part of the book – sister to James and beloved by many strong men. She takes charge and handles many crises that the men around her cannot. She fights to try to save her family's railroad from collapse.

**James (Jim) Taggart:** President of TT and Dagny's elder brother. He is her opposite: lazy and whiny, and tries to keep from making any decisions so no blame can ever be attributed to him. He comes on the scene in the first chapter and we soon know he is up to making any kind of deal with any scum in order to stay rich.

**Henry (Hank) Rearden:** Owner of Rearden Steel and creator of a new and stronger metal: Rearden metal. His Steel mill is mentioned in the first chapter and we are introduced to him in the next. He is a self-made man and proud to work. He is a role model to many other business owners and a great business man. His family mooches off him, none of them doing anything to earn a living.

**Francisco d'Anconia:** A childhood friend of the Taggart children, he is the heir to a copper fortune in Argentina. He is handsome and seems to excel at anything he tries. He has a reputation for making a profit from everything he does. He owns the San Sebastián Mines and seems to be living the life of a playboy and letting his company sink into ruin, yet is a very intelligent man. None of the men in power take him seriously.

**Ragnar Danneskjöld:** A swashbuckling pirate with the looks of a Viking warrior. He seems to have some connection with Francisco. His name is introduced in part one, but we don't get to learn much about him until the later parts of the story. Ragnar is young and brave, yet doesn't want to be a pirate – he wants to be a teacher.

**Eddie Willers:** Is the first character we meet. He is Dagny's assistant at TT and he also grew up with the Taggart children. He and Dagny were friends throughout their lives. He is very loyal to Dagny. While he is not as intelligent as the others, he does know right from wrong and always tries to do right. Yet he cannot seem to make any type of difference in the world. Eddie is in the background of almost all the railroad scenes – the backbone that keeps it all together.

**Orren Boyle:** A competitor of Rearden's who is not talented and not a hard worker. He is introduced in chapter one and is active throughout the book. He stays in competition by bribing officials and eventually taking positions high in the government so he can pass laws that he will benefit from. He seems to be one of James Taggart's best friends. He gets so good at being sly and sneaky that he even starts to blackmail friends as well as enemies.

**Richard Halley:** A composer. His music is used to set the background for many scenes, just as it would be for a movie. He is one of the best modern musicians but he retires early.

**Hugh Akston:** Once a professor at Patrick Henry University – now a cook. He looks on John Galt and his companions as sons.

**Lillian Rearden:** Hank's wife, she schemes to keep the title of wife of the richest industrialist. She uses guilt and lies at every step of her life.

**Philip Rearden:** Hank's brother who lives off his brother's charity. Often seen helping other moochers.

**Moochers and Looters:** A gang of characters who all try to blackmail, pressure or bully others so that they can gain some sort of advantage. None of them do any real work and they are all concerned about not taking any responsibility for any actions.

| | |
|---|---|
| Paul Larkin | Ivy Starnes |
| Wesley Mouch | Mr. Thompson |
| Betty Pope | Kip Chalmers |
| Dr. Robert Stadler | Chick Morrison |
| Dr. Ferris | Mr. Mowen |
| Eugene Lawson | Mr. Meigs |

**Industrialists, Producers and the Talented:** A group
of people who have a talent and work hard at their jobs
– some rich, others just the best at what they do. All are
happy and loving people and all contribute to making
their communities better places within which to live.

| | |
|---|---|
| Owen Kellogg | Gwen Ives |
| Ellis Wyatt | Dwight Sanders |
| Dan Conway | Quentin Daniels |
| Midas Mulligan | Cherryl Brooks |

# Themes in the Book

**Contrasts:** Almost every concept is shown from both sides and to the full extent of what might happen if that concept were followed. This really sets the choices that the characters have to make in sharp relief. The use of the name of a hero of the book, John Galt, is also used to express giving up: "Who is John Galt?"

**Sex:** Contrasted, like everything else. When sex is performed because it is what a character thinks they should do, it is dull and lifeless, soon over and boring. When sex happens because two people admire and respect each other, then it is breathless, joyful and done with no regrets. One is like gulping down medicine to get it over with just to say you did it. The other is like soaring on wings of eagles.

**Physical Descriptions:** These are used to show a person's spirit. The intellectuals often have their heads thrown back or up, look people right in the eye, and sprawl out when relaxing. Tension is in the bodies of the producers – not as a negative, but as a foundation showing that they have the strength to get the job done. Muscles are part of the healthy people. The moochers dart their eyes around, rarely make eye contact and are flabbier. They smile too much, but it is an ugly kind of smile – done not with joy but with pleading/begging. Their faces are described as wrinkled or in shadow. In meeting places, they stick so far to the shadows they can only see black orbs (like a skull) instead of being able to see each other's eyes.

**Buildings and Human Structures:** They are described as noble and often reaching for the sky or with static properties that make them seem to be moving forward.

Sheets of glass are used to show a command of the vista and the world beyond the rooms. Example: the description of Dagny's apartment – two rooms on the top floor of a skyscraper. The sheets of glass in the corner window of her living room made it look like the prow of a ship in motion.

**Moochers:** They are no better than flat-out robbers and thieves, also called the looters. Their call to inaction is to cry, "It's not my fault; I can't be blamed." Their favorite excuse is that conditions and circumstances were absolutely beyond human control, so nothing could have been done to prevent whatever disaster they are in the middle of. Evil is to have no purpose, to be unhappy, to deny the glory of having a mind. There is the possibility for a few who fall into the moochers' world to be unaware of the consequences, to temporarily think that taking things for the good of others is the way to live, that general charity is good. For just a few of these people, it is possible to learn more, to understand they were wrong and to break out of this group, but it is hard.

**Double Talk, Nonsense and bailing out the looters:**
"Dr. Pritchett was telling us that nothing is anything." The looters are shown mucking things up over and over, and the strong few keep bailing them out time after time and making things run on time or work like they should. Still, no thanks is ever given when the day is saved by the strong. Instead, the looters babble about things working out, that things will always work out. The double talk is really highlighted in the foolish names of the laws passed by the looters – meant to be so tame that no one could object, yet hiding the true meaning – *and the same thing is done today!* (Pay attention to the names some political groups and nonprofit groups give themselves.)

**Blood and Arteries:** These are used to describe complex systems such as the railroad or an intricate motor. They are alive with energy, but controlled remotely by a human mind. The body should be looked at like a temple and treated with love, respect and honor.

**Sharing:** The moochers want everyone to share, so they try to convince the entire population that it is a form of loving your fellow man to share wealth and supplies. They corrupt the concept by getting people to just share, sacrifice for others and talk about the good of charity without thinking and without purpose. Yet they do not share or contribute to charities – they hog up everything they can get.

**Human Ability:** In contrast to sharing, human ability is held up to be admired for each individual achievement, promoting pride about anything done well. Individual achievement can be enjoyed by all, but belongs only to the one who created or produced the item in question.

# About The Book

This book was Ms. Rand's third major book, published in 1957. This was still a time when women wore dresses, didn't work and barely had the right to vote, and here we are with a strong woman character in this book who acts like a woman of today would. If it can be imagined, it can be done. This book is still in print today – and, even more impressive, some scholarships to colleges are granted based solely on an essay on this book!

Most people think this book is great, a masterpiece. It did get a large backlash from religious organizations. Although the book doesn't set out as a main or sub-theme that religion is the opiate of the masses, as the communists said, it does have running through it the concept that people and their intelligence and ability are the only things that can bring true inspiration and the only things that should be worshipped.

That connects us to another circumstance of this book: communism was a viable theory for many people when this was published. Many communists were hoping that the USSR would be successful and that the entire world would follow suit. This book was a pushback showing how ridiculous that would be and showing how people cannot give to other people according to what they need if they also take with no regard from those who are producing. It seems history has proven her right, if the breadlines and despair of the USSR in the eighties is anything to go by.

The huge controversy regarding charity is still ongoing among readers of this book. This topic is addressed in the philosophy Ms. Rand created called

"Objectivism" (details below). It is, as the book says, a choice each person has to make, but they have a duty to make it from reasoned ideas – not mushy, unformed and foggy ideas about helping people out. It is interesting to note that Benjamin Franklin had almost the same outlook on charity and his face is on our $1 bill – and the dollar is the symbol the good people in this book use as standing for value, *not* greed.

# About The Author

Ayn Rand was born and raised in Russia. Always intelligent and a quick learner and observer, the Bolshevik Revolution caused her father to lose his pharmacy and the family had periods of near starvation. She defected to America in 1925. She met a man such as she writes about, and married him. This book is dedicated to Frank O'Connor, and they were married for fifty years. She often stressed that people may think there is no real person like her heroes, but she found and married one and knows there are more out there in the world.

Her first book, *The Fountainhead*, was published in 1943. Ayn also wrote and lectured on philosophy, creating her own niche called Objectivism. She called it, "A philosophy for living on earth." There is still an active foundation, the Ayn Rand Institute, which operates on this principle.

"My personal life," says Ayn Rand, "is a postscript to my novels; it consists of the sentence: *'And I mean it.'* I have always lived by the philosophy I present in my books – and it has worked for me, as it works for my characters. The concretes differ, the abstractions are the same." Ms. Rand died in 1982 in her NYC apartment.

## The Basics of Objectivism

*My philosophy, in essence, is the concept of man as a heroic being, with his own happiness as the moral purpose of his life, with productive achievement as his noblest activity, and reason as his only absolute.* —Ayn Rand

Ayn Rand was once asked if she could present the essence of Objectivism while standing on one foot. Her answer was:

1.  Metaphysics: Objective Reality
2.  Epistemology: Reason
3.  Ethics: Self-interest
4.  Politics: Capitalism

She then translated those terms into familiar language:

1.  "Nature, to be commanded, must be obeyed."
2.  "You can't eat your cake and have it too."
3.  "Man is an end in himself."
4.  "Give me liberty or give me death."

The category of Ethics gets beaten up the most, with many thinking we should give out charity to more than just people struck by disaster (i.e., help if a house burns down but not if someone cannot find a house to rent). Here, in a nutshell, is how Objectivism looks at ethics – and why:

"Reason is man's only proper judge of values and his only proper guide to action. The proper standard of ethics is: man's survival qua man – i.e., that which is required by man's nature for his survival as a rational being (not his momentary physical survival as a mindless brute). Rationality is man's basic virtue, and his three fundamental values are: reason, purpose, self-esteem. Man – every man – is an end in himself, not a means to the ends of others; he must live for his own sake, neither sacrificing himself to others nor sacrificing others to himself; he must work for his rational self-interest, with the achievement of his own happiness as the highest moral purpose of his life. Thus, Objectivism rejects any form of altruism – the claim that morality consists in living for others or for society."[1]

1    Rand, Ayn (2005-04-21). Atlas Shrugged: (Centennial Edition). Penguin Group. Kindle Edition.

## Dear Amazon Customer,

Thank you for your purchase. We hope you enjoyed reading the 100-Page Summary of Atlas Shrugged. Our team is dedicated to your satisfaction and we want to know if your expectations were met. If for any reason you are unable to leave a favorable rating on Amazon, please email us at info@pylonpublishing.com. We want to know what we need to do to fix the problem and make a better product for all our readers. Your 100% satisfaction is our responsibility.

You can leave us feedback by following the link below or scan the QR code:

### Review this book on Amazon

http://tinyurl.com/c6npw9o

Thank you and we look forward to hearing from you.
Sincerely,

## Preston
Founder, Pylon Publishing Inc.

Made in the USA
Lexington, KY
18 January 2013